PATIENT OF PATIENCE

PATIENCE TEACHES SILENCE NOT AS WEAKNESS, BUT AS THE FOUNDATION OF TRUE POWER.

ARTIST LAVANYA

Made with ♥ on the Notion Press Platform
www.notionpress.com

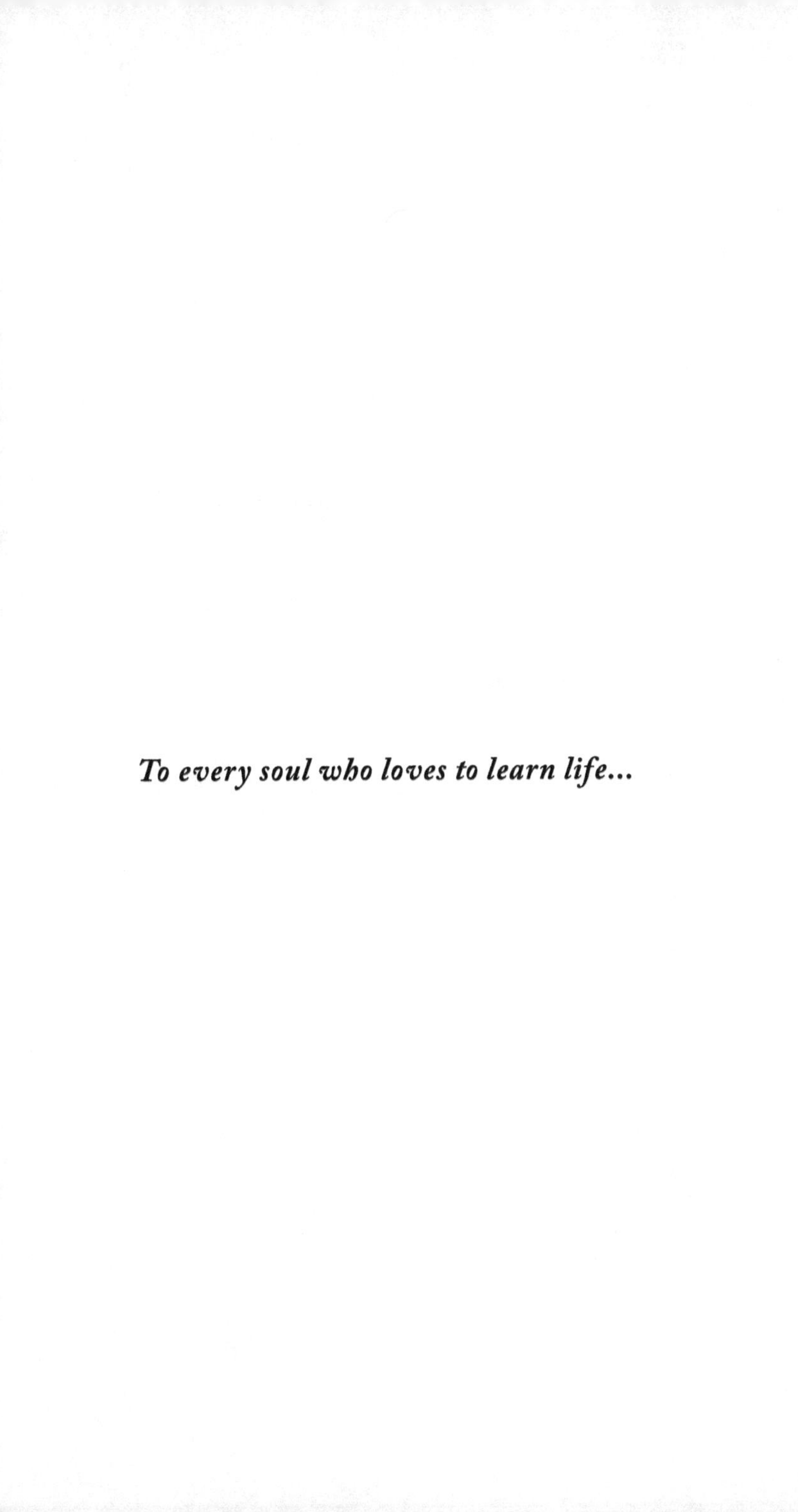

To every soul who loves to learn life...

Contents

Contents

Foreword

A Note from the Author's Sister

As the sister of the author, I've had the privilege of witnessing the journey behind this book unfold up close.

What began as quiet thoughts scribbled in a diary gradually transformed into full chapters, often written late into the night. I've seen the moments of uncertainty, the sparks of inspiration, and the immense care poured into every word on these pages.

This book is more than just a collection of writings—it's a heartfelt expression of my sister's soul. It reflects her passion, perseverance, curiosity, and her sincere desire to make a difference. Whether you're here to reflect, learn, or simply enjoy a thoughtful read, I'm confident you'll find something that resonates with you.

Having always admired her strength and creativity, I couldn't be prouder to share her work with the world. I hope it inspires you as deeply as it has inspired me.

Happy Reading!

Preface

TIME IS POWERFUL

I never expected that a life experience would eventually take shape as a book.

Back when I was in 10th grade, I used to write in a diary. Honestly, I never imagined that one day I would become an author. Then, as I moved into 11th grade, I gradually began writing poems—even without a clear direction. By the time I reached 12th grade and began doing some research, I heard a voice from within that said, "I CAN DO IT." From that moment on, everything else became a matter of time.

It wasn't during a rainy evening or a lazy afternoon that this realization struck—it was a quiet, inner calling that told me there was a story waiting to be shared.

Now, let me tell you why I wrote this book.

In life, some people are able to speak openly and boldly, even in their lowest moments. But there are others who silently carry their pain. I am not one of them. I don't believe in hiding my emotions. For me, the best way to express what I feel is through writing.

Dear Readers,

Thank you for picking up this book.

Here's what brought it to life:

This book is a reflection of fleeting emotions and the many unspoken words that reside in silence. It is designed to help readers enhance their writing skills by using the English language as a tool to express deeply embedded thoughts and experiences.

The poems presented here serve as mirrors to real-life situations, inviting readers to engage in thoughtful and serious reflection. They revolve around themes such as deep affection, success, attachment, silence, and fragmented emotions.

These pieces are meant to resonate with universal sentiments and appeal to contemporary sensibilities. Readers are encouraged to explore the themes with love, vision, and emotional insight—supported by reflection and understanding.

Acknowledgements

First and foremost, I would like to thank my mom, dad, and closest friends for their invaluable feedback and unwavering patience throughout the journey of Patient of Patience. Truly, their belief in this book made all the difference.

A heartfelt thank you to my sister and her friends for their constant support, encouragement, and understanding during the many late nights and early mornings spent working on this project.

To my friends and early readers who offered their thoughts and feedback—your insights played a vital role in shaping this book into what it is today.

And finally, thank you to every reader who picks up this book. Your time, attention, and imagination breathe life into these pages.

Prologue

Patience teaches silence not as weakness, but as the foundation of true power.

They teach us how to run—how to chase dreams, meet deadlines, and race against time.

But waiting?

Waiting is a war of its own—silent, slow, and often cruel in ways most people never notice.

This book may seem simple at first glance, but if you shift your perspective, you'll find there's so much within its pages.

In just a few lines of prose and poetry, you'll discover deeper meanings and quiet truths.

I haven't tried to explain everything—

I've simply captured the whispers of the heart in a handful of words.

1. When the Suppressed Rain Started Flowing

This poem captures the tears that don't fall every day, but when they do, they lighten the heart, just like the rain.

In the tip-tap vibration,
Droplets go up-down
Like tears go underground.
Neither can stop them
Nor can change the direction
of ground.
Rain can quench the exterior fire
Unfitted to fix the inner burn,
Streaming rain sense glacier
In the middle of balmy tears.

This poem reflects the kind of tears that don't fall every day. But when they do, they lighten the heart, just like a gentle rain.

Just as rain occasionally drops from the sky through clouds, tears too are released from the eyes when they can no longer hold the weight of long-standing darkness and blindness —

the kind that settles quietly over the weeks and months.

When the rain begins to fall, everything seems to melt and soften. Everything becomes wet. In the same way, when tears escape the eyes, the brain senses the release of adrenaline and the built-up frustration that has been quietly waiting for release over time.

Rain may soothe the surface, offering a cooling sensation to the body, but it cannot reach deep enough to extinguish the fire that burns within the soul.

However, when tears are finally allowed to fall, they may raise the body's temperature, but they also begin to dissolve the darkness. It feels as though the inner world becomes still and calm.

Sometimes, the rain offers a strange kind of comfort. When we stand beneath the falling droplets, we can hide our tears — not because we want to deceive others, but because we cannot always explain what we feel. And in those moments, the only one we can truly turn to is ourselves.

2. Expectations Hits Worst and Bad

The theme of society's expectations versus my expectations explores the tension between societal norms and personal aspirations. In this poem, I have portrayed what happens when people awaken me under the weight of their expectations—and what unfolds when I begin to expect something from myself.

Their jerk of exceeding expectations Cease my hands,
apart from my expectations
charmingly craft my existence.
They push my legs toward the earth
I look into sky filled
with diamond crumps.
Dazzling light reaches my eyes
when I suffer darkness in dries
which is my own
expectations,
expectations
and expectation.

"Not everybody can do everything , But everybody can do something best"

There are two types of expectations: the ones we have from ourselves, and the ones others have from us.

I believe that my expectations have given me life. When I expect something from myself, it feels as if I've grown fairy wings—wings that allow me to speak freely and give me a sense of liberation.

What I mean is that my expectations fill me with self-love, boost my confidence, motivate me, and push me toward my goals. They ignite a bonfire of passion within me.

But when others begin to pile their expectations on me, it feels like those wings are being clipped. I'm brought back down to the ground, burdened by the weight of fulfilling everyone's wishes and societal norms—norms that once promised to give wings, but now only hold me back.

3. The Peace of Unbroken Silence - Part I

In this poem, you'll explore two contrasting personalities.

I have related human skin tones to various ornaments and adornments.

It reflects how both conventionally beautiful and less appreciated faces often face disrespect—and how they feel and respond to it.

I saw a dazzling
piece of merchandise kept
in the darkness of the almirah.
It's difficult to be out of station
If you're black
and if you're white too.
you have to stay inside
whatever you do,
black doesn't looks good,
whites look so good.

Both make the blend of embarrassment.
In the end, you'll find broke yourself.
they'll taunt

No matter, how much you
crucify yourself on your own.

I've noticed that many of the most beautiful things around me are kept hidden or locked away.

Even when a new set of crockery is brought into the house, it's often not used regularly. Sometimes, it's taken out only for special occasions. On the other hand, if the crockery is unattractive, it's not used when guests visit—because serving with it might be considered disrespectful.

If we look at both situations, we can conclude that beautiful things are often not allowed to be used freely, and the things considered less appealing are also not brought out in front of others.

> *"There is a fear of displaying beautiful things, lest they be stolen, and a fear of revealing the ugly, lest they be disgraced."*

I've simply borrowed this example from non-living things—objects without a soul—because they can no longer feel. But this poem is meant for the living, for those who can feel deeply and intensely.

So, what about them?

Neither someone considered "ugly" is allowed to step out freely, nor someone extraordinarily beautiful—like the

Kohinoor—is granted that freedom. If someone is too beautiful, they're hidden away for fear of being stolen or harmed by the evil eye. And if someone is seen as unattractive, they are shamed or kept out of sight.

Who gave society the power to decide this for us?

Who allowed such racial or appearance-based discrimination?

No one. No one ever said that beauty or lack of it should be a reason to confine someone.

This cage of judgment, this constant boredom caused by restrictions, needs to be broken.

Everyone has their dreams and standards. Everyone deserves the chance to enjoy life on their terms.

4. The Peace of Unbroken Silence - Part II

In this poem, I have expressed my love and faith with silence.

Silence was near
when I was there,
Silence is here
when I am here,
I hope it will furthermore together,
when I will gather.
Thoughts are accomplished
when I diminished my company.
Silence is my hobby
when everyone becomes creepy.
I love silence
when no one loves mankind,
I love silence
when everyone hates my mind.
Silence is my perfect ship
when no one trusts my voyage.
I love silence in adventures
even in drastic ventures.

True strength often comes from silence.

Sometimes, it's better to remain silent than to try to make someone understand.

Even our scriptures advise us to invest our time and energy only in those who value our words and genuinely try to understand us. Otherwise, all our efforts go in vain, and our knowledge loses its worth.

I've learned to embrace the power of silence since childhood. But that doesn't mean I'm an introvert. People often call me an extraordinary extrovert because I talk a lot. However, I choose silence in moments when I feel the person in front of me won't understand or isn't interested in listening.

I prefer staying calm in places where I don't feel respected or welcomed. I observe the person in front of me, understand their behavior, and respond accordingly. Because if someone isn't even willing to listen, then you're not just wasting your words—you're also wasting your time and energy.

5. A White Night

This poem is about the relaxation of the mind that the soul seeks for.

Need a dark night to walk,
winter nights to explore,
cool waves to heal my halk
and a seat for freshness and flores.
That night I would lockdown
the barrier to stop the traffic rush,
and will cage those heart-piercing
fires and crush.

That night I'll cease
my arenaline to shout,
and will stop my curious
mental status to mount.

"I am not afraid of the battlefield, I am just afraid of the
path where people walk after loosing themselves"

Sometimes, our mind and soul crave peace — the kind of peace that can cool the mind and extinguish the fire burning within the body.

There are moments when I just want to leave everything behind and escape to a quiet place where I can simply be with myself and my silence. A place where no one offers empty consolation or tries to wipe away my tears.

I long to sit in a peaceful corner, alone, and cry — to release all the frustration and chaos from my mind and soul.

Sometimes, I wish for a cold winter night with empty roads, no traffic, and no noise. I want to stand in the middle of that quiet road and scream — scream until everything I've held inside is free. I'd put up a barrier, not to push people away, but to finally let myself feel, uninterrupted.

Let the cold wind calm me instead of anyone's presence. Let each tear slowly turn into vapor, drifting away with the breeze, until my mind is quiet, and my heart feels light and empty — finally at peace.

6. Psychic View of Outer Faces

This poem reveals the secret hidden behind silence.
What lies within the hearts of those who seem rude?
What thoughts do they carry deep inside?

I KNOW YOU DO NOT CARE...
BUT YOU DO NOT..?
I meditate that your inner soul needs deep affection,
that are faded by around.
An affection that can cure your scars...

WHAT ABOUT SENTIMENTS?
ARE YOU EGOCENTRIC?
LITERALLY?
Just the matter is that
mankind didn't care about your emotions,
that now it set off as a bomb which is
named as self-centered.

YOU ARE SO HOSTILE..
SERIOUSLY..?
NE'ER

It's just the running inner traffic
in which abundant state of affairs
are suffered and jammed.

WHY ARE YOU QUIET ALWAYS?

You are not
you are sustaining millions of vocals
behind the agreement with face,
however furthermore you register
in you mind that-
No one cares,
No one cares
and No one cares.

Silence is the best answer ever.

Every person has their struggles in life—challenges they often cannot share with anyone, and that others may never fully understand. Sometimes, however, these struggles become visible—reflected in a person's expression or hidden in their words. Yet instead of trying to understand what might be wrong, people often rush to criticize the behavior of someone who is already hurting.

They immediately begin questioning us for our actions, without even once trying to accept or understand our behavior. They walk away without giving it a thought. How much better it would be if, just once, someone asked with kindness and patience what was truly going on. How comforting it would be for a sad soul to find support in someone's words.

But in today's world, people rarely pause—even for a moment—to consider what someone else might be going through or what circumstances they might be stuck in.

"Always try to use positive words wherever you go."

7. A Long Sleep

Sometimes I wish to go into such a deep sleep where I can drown all my troubles and become crisis-free.

I want to go on a long sleep
in which I could forget to weep,
I could forget to laugh,
and forget to calm.
In which I wish I could find my craft
and lost my raft.
I could live in a room
with my dreamy roof,
with the ceiling of flying kites,
and in which I could ignore
all my unwanted life.
I wish I could have everything
on my palm,
Even the switch of disturb and laugh
and the map of my craft
and a joyous path.

A LONG SLEEP — Solely Dedicated to the Fiction of My Dream Life.

Sometimes, we all long for a deep, uninterrupted sleep — a long sleep where we are in complete control. A place where no one can bother or console us. A quiet space where we can create our way of living.

There are times when we want to laugh and feel happy, but the complications of life make it difficult. So, we often wish that things could happen our way, or that we could escape for a while into our dreams, where everything unfolds according to our desires.

Just like an artist who makes puppets dance to their tune, we too wish to become the master of our lives — to take charge without interference.

I often feel like disappearing to a distant island, where I lose my raft and live the rest of my days in peace, away from all the noise and chaos. It's not that I don't want to live — I do. But the freedom to live fully and freely is missing. At times, it feels like we're simply exhausted from constantly enduring life's harsh realities.

8. Regret For..?

Every day is a new beginning, so what should I regret it for?

I am not, what I react
what I react, I am not.
What I was
I am not,
What I am
I was not.
Then why do I feel regret for?
What I am ...or
what I was...
Why stress for?
while having the same time,
same rights, and same way of dying.
Why feel sad in the end for?
If had fun with the drape
of fake lace...
If had fun with a cheerful glance.

Why Regret For?

This poem reflects the question—why do I worry?

If you look closely, there are many reasons to worry. But when we have only one life, and in the end, we all return to ashes, then why should I worry?

We are not always what we appear to be. Sometimes we laugh a lot, but behind those laughs hides a sadness buried deep in our hearts and souls.

Pain isn't always visible on the forehead as worry lines—sometimes it cuts like a dagger through the heart.

Yet, we often regret the past that is no longer with us.

Or we regret the present that might not be there tomorrow.

So, again—why regret?

9. Route Least to be Depressed

This poem is dedicated to those kind-hearted souls whose demise would turn humanity to dust.

One day I'll shut down my eyes
and off my existence insight.
I'll cage my heart-piercing sounds
and open my mind to the clouds.
I'll get neutralized
no emotions to be crazy,
and sense to be lazy,
that day I'll tie my feet
for stopping myself
to run at the roof to jump
though riding without
landing parachute
ans wrong stupe.
I'll shrink all my toxify blood
from the heart that stops the routes
to flow in the body moves.
and will switch off my body,
pat my head to the spirit of soul

and a route to heaven on a free wall.

People with soft hearts often find it difficult to say no.
They tend to share their emotions openly, without considering whether the other person is deserving of such vulnerability. Sometimes we express our pain or sorrow to someone who may misuse it — and later, we regret it deeply.

When this happens repeatedly, the mind begins to feel weary. We could say it starts to consume itself. Gradually, the heartbeat continues, but only mechanically — not enough to make someone truly feel alive.

This poem has two layers. The first speaks of a kind of death that isn't physical — it's the death of emotion. When a person loses their ability to feel, they also lose a part of their humanity. And without humanity, a person becomes nothing more than a fragile skeleton that could break at any moment. Sometimes, we start believing that this world isn't worthy of our goodness. So we suppress it. We bury our kindness, and people begin to misunderstand us or speak negatively about us. But they fail to realize that they are the very reason behind this transformation.

Eventually, even the blood seems to stop flowing from the heart. That pure-hearted soul, broken by the weight of the world, quietly returns to the soil — and their soul ascends to peace.

If this continues, a time may come when no good people are left, and with them, humanity itself will vanish.

10. Toxic World

Sometimes, we have to let go of the habits and people who bring us sorrow and pain. In this poem, I have offered a glimpse into their presence and how they were dealt with.

Many times we have to give up
unhealthy foods which cause
harm to the body.
Acidic foods often leave a spatter
that may be so stubborn which
cannot be cured even when
escorted by the doctor's prescription.
Glossy oily foods may hurt,
may it be ruined
that it will melt your heart.
Hot food may burn you
in the fire of the red flame.
which can leave it's impact
even after being estinguishing.
Fake colours in the food can
leave spots in the inner soul.

"Just once, everyone should take advice from someone who has faced failure, because only that person can truly teach you where not to make mistakes."

This poem is dedicated to toxic people.

In it, I've drawn a comparison between unhealthy food habits and the negative behavior of certain individuals.

Death doesn't always come from poor eating habits or an unhealthy lifestyle — sometimes, it's the soul that suffers. It begins to fade because of the cruelty and mistreatment of others.

Sometimes, we must walk away from those who leave a damaging impact on our minds and hearts.

There is still time...

Some people leave behind such deep wounds with their fiery words that they never fully heal. And even if they do, they leave scars — marks that no one else can erase.

There are times when people say things so subtly, yet so sharply, that we're left speechless. We can't respond, nor can we carry the heavy burden of their words.

The fire in certain words can be so destructive that even trying to extinguish it doesn't erase its damage.

Stains of some colors remain on clothes — but worse are the stains left on our character. Words and actions, when poisonous, can leave lasting marks not just on the outside, but deep within.

11. Patience with Hidden Venue

This poem is dedicated to all the girls who struggle and work hard to make their parents proud, even in the most unfavorable and challenging conditions.

I saw her balmy tears
in the thickness of eyewear,
I saw the marks of tears
in the pillow of nights, she wears...
I saw her hustle
between the notebook
and the invisible covers,
I saw the invisible ones
where she kept her book
and lock herself
in the middle maze of the page.
I saw her soft chambers
behind the brittle vocals
and a broken phrase.

This poem, as well as this chapter, is dedicated to girls.

It's not that I support gender discrimination—my intention is only to express what I truly feel.

Being a boy is not easy. They carry the weight of responsibilities from a young age. But at the very least, boys are allowed to live and breathe without constant restrictions.

Girls, on the other hand, are often not even allowed that freedom. Boys can do things with ease, without seeking anyone's permission, and girls must ask for approval at every step. Whether they say it or not, this constant need for permission hurts them deeply.

I've seen girls cry over things that may seem small to others, but there's always a reason behind those tears. I've witnessed how they're blamed or punished over minor issues, how they slowly start to suppress their emotions, burying their dreams and feelings inside.

So if someday a girl appears to be very happy, try asking her how she truly feels. And if you can't ask, just notice the drop of water rolling down her glass—it might not be from the sky but from her heart.

And if you can't understand that either, then look at the tear-soaked pillow she rests her head on each night. And if even that remains unseen, listen carefully to the sharp, bitter words she sometimes speaks—because pain has its way of finding a voice.

12. Whom I Talk with?

This poem is for those people to whom we confide, considering them our own, but who end up taking unfair advantage of us.

Whom I talk with..?...with air..
That wave my way
what I say
in a different clay.
Whom I talk with..?..with vase..
that will break
it's glass
in a single squall.
Whom I talk with..?..with water..
whose depth will
wept the sense
and rinse my whole self.
Whom I talk with..?..with ice..
that freezes my thesis
in a thick molded dice
and keep aside.

When we are emotional, we often speak directly from the heart—without thinking, and without considering whether the person in front of us is even worthy of hearing those words. That is why we are taught not to say anything in moments of extreme happiness or deep sorrow, because in such states, our vulnerability may be taken advantage of.

Sometimes, out of compulsion, we open up to someone who then twists our words and spreads them like the wind to others. What was once a small concern suddenly becomes a topic of wide discussion. At other times, we share our worries with people who don't harm us intentionally, but end up hurting themselves by taking our words too deeply to heart. They carry our pain within them and become burdened by it—and then we feel guilty for troubling someone else with our emotions.

There are also times when we confide in people who neither try to understand us nor offer comfort. Instead, they respond insensitively, behave coldly, or even belittle our concerns, making us feel worse than before.

> "*A person who is defeated is called a loser, But the one who knows how to stand back up after defeat is truly victorious. No one is interested in your struggle or story — unless you win.*"

13. Noiseless Paws

This poem is dedicated to my dog, Roxy, who has shown more loyalty than most human beings.

In our moments of sorrow, she was always the one who stood by us, even before anyone else.

But when it was my turn to be there for her, I found myself helpless...

Knowing that her time was near, I couldn't do anything.

All I'm left with now is regret — and more regrets.

The day 30th June
she ceased to be one,
she came into our existence
like she is something to us.
She started treating us
like she is the only one.
The way she used to wait
for us on the doorstep,
like she is waiting for god step.
In our crises, she couldn't say anything
but she had always stood ahead of us
and fought against the invisible ones.
In simple words, when the whole world

left us,
she was with us.
Now, the speed of paws has slowed
down a bit.
Her fascination has diminished a bit
now, she stopped talking
as she calms down her speed
with swelling feet.

This chapter is dedicated to my dog, Roxy — who never left our side but stood by us, fighting alongside us through every crisis until her very last breath.

When the whole world turned its back on us, she stood like a warrior, as if God had sent us a divine gift — a messiah in the form of unconditional love. But when it was her turn to be helped, we found ourselves helpless. Even though we wanted to save her, it felt like her time had come to return to God. All we could do was mourn and pray for her salvation, hoping that if she is reborn, she finds her way back to us.

She was the only one who used to wait for me at the doorstep as if waiting for God himself. She wouldn't even take a single bite of food until I returned home. That kind of loyalty is rare in today's world. If I truly understand what loyalty means, it is only because of Roxy.

She behaved as though I was her entire world — sharing in my sorrow, rejoicing in my happiness. I still can't understand how time flew by so fast. It's true what they say: good times pass in the blink of an eye, while hard times seem to stretch on endlessly.

In earlier days, she would play with me, teasing me as I'd try to take the leaflet tied around her neck. But as time passed, she slowly withdrew — as if God was gently calling her away from the attachments of this world. Eventually, both her legs gave out. She stopped walking and began counting her final breaths.

That was the greatest loss of my life.

14. Beloved

This poem is dedicated to those who are the backbone of our lives, whose presence is essential to our very existence.

They convey their affection
by hugging them..
The procedure I pick
to convey mine
is prove them.
Sometimes the back bone isn't
on the side of the back,
perhaps it could be one's temperament
whoever supports but shows viz blank.
Sometimes the supporting hand
we all require isn't financially
it's mentally.

Some people are very important in our lives, we could even say they are our soulmates, connected to us through bonds from a previous life. These people are truly special. Their presence feels different, it brings comfort and positivity, like the first light of dawn after a long, dark night.

In the same way, our parents hold a sacred place in our hearts. They are always there to support us. And then comes a time when, as children, it becomes our responsibility to make them proud, to achieve something so meaningful that their pride rises even higher than their stature.

15. Now, Impossible to Relieve

This poem depicts the condition that many times we wish to go back in our life not to change anything but to feel some few moments twice.

The spending day was yesterday
the coming day is the future..and
today is the present day.
can't feel the same moments twice,
can't feel the same feeling twice,
can't illustrate the situation.
Sometimes I wish I could go back in my life
not to change anything,
but to feel some few moments twice.
I am blurred and my gut
has nothing to express,
nor anything to impress
only regrets and regrets.
I thought of having a few more memorable
moments furthermore
but sadly, I can just think of it.
now, haven't idea about the future,

have regretted the past
so, I have only today's present time to
overcome, enjoy, and laugh.

Yesterday has passed, and I am living in today, yet I find myself longing to relive those moments once more.

I want to stop worrying about the world and what people might say — I need to live again, this time for myself.

What I couldn't do yesterday, I must do now. Time passed so quickly, that I don't even know how it slipped away. Those precious moments faded slowly and disappeared.

Now, all I have are the memories, and it is through those moments that this book was born.

I hope to experience such moments again in the future, though I don't know what lies ahead or what destiny holds for me.

16. Want to Live

In this poem, I have expressed the life I want to live and how I wish to take care of myself in today's fast-paced world.

Sometimes I wish I could live
a day filled with peace
no boundaries of sorrow,
no doubt about myself
just self-love, self-care,
self-obsessions and more.
I don't live overlong
A day in which I found myself
happy with an empty mind
No thoughts about hypocrites
meanwhile a laugh at the right time...
That day I wanna live with
Lovely kites who will treat
me like I am bright.
On that day I wanna drape
myself with the wings of
happy white fur and want to eat
sweet caramel with chocolate syrup.

First, Life Painted Me — Now, I am Repainting Myself.

When we go through a lot in life, we often hold on to the hope that one day, everything will be okay — that a moment of peace will arrive. Just like morning follows the darkest night, there are moments of calm that give us strength to keep going.

After the rush of daily life, I often wish for a day off — a chance to go somewhere, breathe freely, or simply take care of myself. In the same way, I long for moments free from the pressures of life. Moments that belong only to me. Moments where no one speaks about me — neither in praise nor criticism.

I wish for a time when people see not just my flaws, but my efforts and achievements too.

On that day, I will truly listen to myself, and follow my heart, and in just one day, I'll begin to lift the weight that has silently been resting on my shoulders.

17. Downfall

This poem presents a moment that comes into the life of every person who struggles — as if time itself must test them at least once.

Why am I stuck?
Why does it seem depressed...?
I am trying to climb
But the longer I climb
The longer I fall...
Does time examine my tolerance?
If so, then why does it demolish me for -
Checking my patience...or
Something a lot...
Sometimes it gives the impression
of being disturbed after grasping around each
one possesses pleasure...
But my intramural moments
Are feeling fallen from overlong...
Don't know what will happen...
Will the future improve through today's hard work
Or, will today be drained by future tension...

Sometimes, there comes a point in life when nothing makes sense, and everything feels confusing. Our hard work seems to go in vain. We feel overwhelmed by pressure, and tears begin to fall. The more we try to do well, the more worthless we start to feel. At times, it feels like the universe is testing us — questioning whether we truly deserve the place or success we dream of.

It's especially disheartening when, during our struggle, we see people who don't put in much effort still doing just fine, while we work hard even for small things and still face setbacks. In those moments, our thoughts begin to shift. Some people give up, but others choose to push forward.

And the ones who move forward have already won — because they've learned to control their heart and mind. They adapt, they grow stronger, and they begin to face challenges with a calm resilience.

18. Sweetness of Hateness

This poem reflects how people become jealous when someone works hard and achieves success.

They see what I am doing
But they don't see
"How I am doing"
They count
No. of notes I earn, Unfitted to count
No. of nights I burn...
They pay me for my work
And not them...
Is there anything special about me?
If...then why this jealousy for
What you are..or
What you are not...

People put aside their passion for the world, I left the world aside for passion.

Many questions will be raised when you dare to dream.

They'll try to manipulate you, to pull you down — not because you're wrong, but because they don't want you to move forward.

People can be strange.

If you do nothing, they say you're not capable of doing anything. But if you achieve something big, they become jealous.

They never see the hard work, the countless efforts behind the scenes — they only notice the result.

They count the money I've earned, but they can't count the nights I spent awake to earn it.

No one acknowledges the silent sacrifices behind success.

Sometimes, I wonder — are they upset with me or with themselves?

And if they're not upset with anyone at all, then where does this jealousy come from?

19. Blend of Some Smack

In this poem, I explore the diverse preferences of different individuals.

Some find happiness in smiles,
Some are happy with every smile.
Some sleep deep in a free yawn,
Some industrious knit their dreams
with the wool of nights and sleepy eyes...
Some are powerless to explore delighting
moments in the kingdom of heaven,
Some are joyous and blissful in the valley of desolation..
Sometimes the fire of burning flames
remains inside...
But splatter of burner boils
And throughout through the throat.

Some carry bundles of melancholy sadness
That they gallop reached through their eyes...
They're happy inside,
They're happy outside,
May it be named as the affair of controversy...

There are all kinds of people in this world, each with a different mindset. Some can remain happy even in sorrow, while others struggle to find joy even in moments of happiness. There is a significant difference between the two. At times, some people find reasons to smile even during hardship, while others manage to find sorrow during celebration. That's why blaming the atmosphere or circumstances is simply a way of giving the mind an excuse. In the end, you do what you choose to do. It's up to you whether you want to be happy or sad.

> *"Yes, sometimes we indeed struggle to feel happy because of old wounds. But the real path to victory lies in healing those wounds and moving forward.*
>
> *Some people experience happiness through favorable circumstances, while others push through even the toughest times. Those who strive for success often don't know what the outcome will be—they simply keep working hard so that, in the end, they have no regrets. And that's what mindset is all about."*

20. Isn't the Art of Letting Go

Sometimes we make mistakes that haunt us for the rest of our lives. This poem is based on that very feeling.

Hard to console
Until I remove my soul,
Hard to accept
Was my mistake
Or a black hole.
Hard to erase those neurons
And fill the heart holes
With my moments furthermore.
I am weaving
The thread of grief
In my subconscious feed,
I am waiting for the moment
I would deed
To remove the curse
From my pleat.

Childishness from the outside and maturity from the inside is the best composition.

Sometimes, we make a mistake so heavy that we carry its regret until the end of our lives.

No matter how much time passes, we are unable to fill the emptiness that others have left inside us because of it. The reason behind that regret may vary — what troubles you might be different from what troubles me.

At times, we can't even share that inner void with anyone. We just keep burying it deep within ourselves. That mistake may happen knowingly, unknowingly, or simply as a consequence of time — a pull that we keep getting drawn toward, unable to resist.

Eventually, we start to feel as if that mistake was a crime. And in that belief, we get swept away by the current of our thoughts, sinking deeper into the river of guilt we've created ourselves.

21. Relationship of Soul with Colors

This poem is dedicated to artists. It reflects an artist's love for colors and the soulful connection they share with their art.

In the liquid of my colorful soul
There are pigments of art.
Flutter in my entire body
As a cluster of dances.
I intake oxygen with soulful beliefs
As like the blissful blessings of God
I had deed.
Art is a fruitful gift
of my scary nights,
Whatever I have all about those flights.

Art is a gift, I gave to myself.

This chapter is dedicated to artists, or rather to anyone who loves colors.

It explores how an artist becomes immersed in colors—without even realizing it. Their passion grows so deeply that colors become a part of their soul. Though people may criticize or question this obsession, the artist's hand still reaches for the palette, even when they try to resist.

For an artist, acrylics and oil paints are like a personal rainbow. As these colors come into their life, everything begins to glow. The world around them becomes vibrant, and in that glow, the artist finds light and meaning.

22. Feelings Aren't Meant to Be Felt

Dedicated to every soul whose emotions have been erased.

Shall I express?
Shall I be silent?
Or stop me from getting violent.
Would be good to cage
The heart's range?
What if I close the door in the coffin's core,
And forget the code.
Though lost my lock mode,
Will they recall my feelings anymore?
Or just let it be what I spoke?
What if I'll be there
With an empty form,
And clear skin,
With a burned sore?
What if I flush all the mercy flooms,
And leave the heart without a porous way to go into?
Will they try
To refill,
Or just use it in a study—

A different thesis?

The ability to speak several languages is an asset, but the ability to remain silent in any language is truly priceless.

Sometimes, I find myself confused—should I open my heart or stay calm, express anger or remain silent? But when I look around and realize that this world often doesn't value genuine love and affection, I feel it's better to stay quiet.

In today's world, people who speak too much—whether they're right or wrong—are often judged quickly and harshly. So, it's wiser to remain silent until there's a real need to speak. Never offer advice unless someone genuinely asks for it. Only those who have lived through such experiences can understand this kind of wisdom.

I, too, was once the kind of person who responded to kindness with even greater kindness. While some admired this trait, others took it as a weakness. With time, I learned to speak only when necessary. This shift brought a positive outcome—it led me to pour my emotions into writing rather than words.

23. Let Me Free

Just me and my freedom.

I am pleased to be free,
Even getting the right of glee,
Want to be grief-free?
But now, how can I be?..
Want to wear
Denim bottom,
Upper cotton.
A cap to cover the head,
And shoes to walk in dome damp.
I want to fly from the mountains
And dip of water
That ocean contains.
Want to out
That shout,
That I keep inside my mouth
Since childhood douth.

I don't want to beat someone, I just only want to win.

I want to be free.
I want to break the cage like a bird.
I want to dance.
I want to celebrate the joys of my journey.
I want to be happy when I think.
I don't want any reason to laugh.
I want to lose myself in the mountains.
I want to bathe in the rivers.
I want to complete my dreams by spreading my wings.
I want to see life closely.
I don't want anyone's permission.
I don't want anyone's shackles.
I don't want anyone's support.
I want the edge of the world.
I just want my love and the company of my triumph.

❧❧❧

"No one can stop me from flying. I don't give anyone the right to stop my wings.
I haven't given this right to even myself."

24. Moist Regrets

Sometimes, we carry a past that we regret, and it continues to disturb our present life.

I have a regret past
And the unforgettable laugh,
That I had lost
In the agony of my yelling last.
Lens of eyes falls out
Seems getting uncomfortable
With stored toxins of life
That embedded in cries.
Clothes in my eyes
Helps in wiping my water lines,
That holds the pressure of heart
And a disturbing life.

25. A Relief of Fever

I need a fever to heal myself.

I want to live my feverish behavior
In the absence of shouting heartaches
With the rivers of garlands from the eyes
And harsh cries.
During I would ignore
All my regrets and unwanted life,
I would vacuum my over-tended mind
And an over-pampered lifestyle.
I would get the prescription
and therapy to heal my hush
For Overcome the laugh
To heal my scars.

When you follow time, time starts following you too.
Sometimes, we long for a fever when we get tired of our
daily routine. In those moments, we crave a break a little
peace which often comes only when we fall slightly ill. That
weariness brings an unexpected sense of relief.

In the same way, I, too, wish for a fever in my life — one that allows me to release all my anger and become free from tension. My mind has started to grow weary, it has started losing hope.

Now, I just wish for a wave to come and wash away all the problems. That wave can be anything — for each person, it might be something different. It could be someone who helps you understand, or simply something that brings calm to your restless mind.

> *"I'm searching for the wings that bring me away from the captivity of this world."*

26. Teenage

This poem is solely dedicated to teenagers, as this phase marks a new beginning in life.

It's the matter of thoughts
And distractive roads,
In which you find people and lose.
It is the simpler way to explore,
And the harder way to roar.
It's the age to grow
And blow the childhood flow.
It's the age of active mood swings
And vague of wings and rings.
That demands freedom,
Even hard redeem.

Everyone walks on the main road, but only a few truly know how to walk carefully on the right path.

Teenage is a phase when a child takes their first step toward a new path. At this stage, the child is often unaware of the ways of the world. It is a time that demands great understanding and awareness, as the journey ahead is filled with challenges.

Some may stumble along the way, but only those with strong determination and a careful approach are able to reach their goals.

Connect With Me

Thank you for taking the time to read Patient of Patience.

If my words resonated with you, inspired you, or simply made you pause and reflect, I would love to hear from you.

Feel free to reach out, share your thoughts, or just say hello. Your messages, feedback, and support truly mean the world to me and keep me going as a writer.

Email: the.embedded.dreams@gmail.com

Instagram: @the_embedded_dreams

Let's stay connected and keep the conversation going—Because every voice matters, and every story deserves to be heard.